nunchaku and sai

nunchaku and sai

Ancient Okinawan Martial Arts

by Ryusho Sakagami

JAPAN PUBLICATIONS, INC.

Published by
JAPAN PUBLICATIONS, INC., Tokyo

Distributors:
UNITED STATES: *Kodansha International/USA, Ltd., through Harper & Row, Publishers, Inc., 10 East 53rd Street, New York, New York 10022.* SOUHT AMERICA: *Harper & Row, Publishers, Inc., International Department.* CANADA: *Fitzhenry & Whiteside Ltd., 150 Lesmill Road, Don Mills, Ontario M3B 2T6.* MEXICO AND CENTRAL AMERICA: *HARLA S. A. de C. V., Apartado 30–546, Mexico 4, D. F.* BRITISH ISLES: *International Book Distributors Ltd., 66 Wood Lane End, Hemel Hempstead, Herts HPZ 4RG.* EUROPEAN CONTINENT: *Boxerbooks, Inc., Limmatstrasse 111, 8031 Zurich.* AUSTRALIA AND NEW ZEALAND: *Book Wise (Australia) Pty. Ltd., 104–8 Sussex Street, Syndey 2000.* THE FAR EAST AND JAPAN: *Japan Publications Trading Co., Ltd., 1–2–1, Sarugaku-cho, Chiyoda-ku, Tokyo 101.*

First printing: November 1974
Seventh printing: October 1981

ISBN 0-87040-333-8

Photographs by Hideo Matsunaga
Printed in U.S.A.

Preface

In contrast to karate, which has been steadily gaining popularity all over the world for the past few decades, the ancient martial arts of Okinawa (*Okinawa Kobudo*) have, for lack of instructors and people to carry on the tradition, receded and were at one time in danger of being almost totally forgotten. But they are one wing of the same system from which karate developed and have indeed been the basis on which karate has grown. The two—ancient Okinawan martial arts and karate—are like wheels at the opposite end of the same axle. It is clearly a mistake, therefore, to consider karate to be the only Okinawan martial art.

It is a very fortunate thing that, in more recent years, the and persevering efforts of many martial arts masters, are being reappraised. Their true values are beginning to be understood by many people, including those engaged in the study of karate. I personally am very happy to see this turn in events. The efforts of people carrying out this kind of study can help deepen the general understanding of all martial arts, both modern and ancient. In addition, such study can help in developing the spiritual personalities of martial arts students, can introduce the ancient martial arts to the world, and can become a field worthy of inclusion in educational programs at all levels.

In connection with this study, all of us concerned with the ancient martial arts of Okinawa owe a debt of gratitude to the late Shinken Taira, who developed the foundation on which all future work in the field must proceed. This book is one part of that work, and in its production and publication a number of persons have contributed valuable time, talent, and effort. I should like to express my gratitude to the men who performed the techniques shown in the photographs: my son Sadaaki Sakagami, Shigeo Yamada, and Miss Kimiko Yanagisawa. For their encouragement and assistance I thank Iwao Yoshizaki, Managing Director of Japan Publications, and Toshihiro Kuwahara, who was directly responsible for the editorial and production work on the book. Finally, I should like to thank Hideo Matsunaga who took the photographs.

September, 1974

Ryusho Sakagami

Contents

Historical Background

By the words *Ancient Okinawan Martial Way* (*Okinawa Kobudo*), I refer to those martial arts that, in contrast to karate, which is as its name implies performed with empty (*kara*) hands (*te*), employ various weapons. The ancient, armed, martial arts, a part of the larger Okinawan system to which karate too belongs, make use of a number of distinctive weapons of kinds unusual in the rest of the world. Some of them are the *bo*, the *sai*, the *tonfa*, the *nunchaku*, and the *nicho gama*. I shall discuss these in more detail later. As is true in the case of karate as well, there is little documentary evidence concerning the history of the older martial arts. It is certain, however, that the geographical location and other characteristics of Okinawa and the other Ryukyu Islands played an important role in their development, as in other aspects of the history of the Ryukyu people.

There are more than sixty large and small islands in the Ryukyu chain, which stretches along a belt of the Pacific ocean centering on the twenty-sixth parallel of north latitude. Okinawa, the major island in the group, is 500 kilometers from Kyushu, the southernmost of the major Japanese islands; 600 kilometers from Taiwan; and 800 kilometers from Foochow on the Chinese mainland. Since the islands are in the subtropical zone, the trees and other plants retain their lush green foliage the year round.

From ancient times, Okinawa has been the artistic, cultural, and martial heart of the islands. All of the leading centers of the island are located in its southern part: Shuri, the ancient capital of the Ryukyu kingdom; Naha, the most important port for international trade; Tomari, the most important domestic transportation center and the location of a thriving salt-producing industry; and Kumemura, the location of a settlement of immigrants from China.

This last village and the Chinese who lived there are intimately related to the development of both karate and the ancient Okinawan martial arts. Unfortunately, however, it is impossible to explain the process of this development in detail because of the scarcity of documentary evidence. In all of the martial arts, there is a strong tendency to rely on word-of-mouth transmission for the passing of information from one generation to another; and in Okinawan martial arts this tendency is especially pronounced. The scarcity of such material was aggravated by the violent fighting and burning that took place on Okinawa in World War II. Nonetheless, using the small amount of written material that is available and relying heavily on the verbal teachings of older people, one can make some general statements about the history of the ancient Okinawan martial arts. Though the documents about them have been scattered and lost, the techniques themselves have been passed down intact.

The first historical mention of Okinawa occurs in the Chinese document known as the *Sui Shu*, which was written in the Chinese dynastic history of the Sui period (581–618) which shows that the people of Okinawa were engaging in intercourse with the peoples of other lands in the sixth century A.D. Another Chinese document called the *Yuan-shi Liu-ch'iu Ch'uan* says that, even several centuries ago, it was possible to travel by ship from the Ryukyus to Foochow in about six days. Obviously, Okinawan people were in contact with China and her ancient culture. In addition, they carried on trade and other affairs with Korea and Japan as well, though the prevalence of pirates in the waters off Japan probably served as an obstacle in the path of closer relations in that quarter.

Still, it is known that thirty people from the southern islands—they were called the

Yakushima people—brought tribute to the Japanese court in 616 A.D. Such tribute voyages seem to have continued until the middle of the Nara period (646–794). In those times, each of the Ryukyu islands was a governmental entity unto itself. The products that they had to offer other countries in trade were fruits and sea products, a small amount of sulfur, abaca cloth, and whetstones. Almost completely lacking mineral resources, the islands were forced to turn to other nations in trade for such materials.

In the tenth century, when he was only fifteen years old, a boy named Sonton, said to be a descendant of Minamoto Tametomo, a member of the famous Genji clan, became lord of Urasoe and then proceeded to unite the islands into a nation and to become its king. The dynasty established by this enterprising man lasted for seventy three years, but ultimately power fell to another family. The kings of the next dynasty brought the various lords of the nation under their dominion, stimulated trade with foreign nations in an attempt to strengthen the economy, and—it is said—forbade the use of arms. This last measure may have acted as a great stimulus to the development of Okinawan martial arts like karate, in which ordinary military weapons are not used. The policy of forbidding arming of the people was possibly strengthened when the islands passed into the control of the Japanese Shimazu family of Kyushu, in 1609.

There is a tradition, however, to the effect that neither the native Okinawan governments nor the Japanese Shimazu ever forbade the use of weapons and that their lack in the Ryukyus is to be explained by the scarcity of workable metals in the islands. It is likely that iron was being imported into.Okinawa as early as the sixth century. Chinese envoys sent to Okinawa during the Ming dynasty reported on their return to China that among the local people iron pots and other metal articles of daily use were more popular than such luxuries as fine silks. Furthermore, it is known that the government of Okinawa established a portside office for the control of iron to be used in the manufacture of agricultural implements.

Some of the Chinese envoys who came to the Ryukyus remained for a long time. The groups sent by the Ming dynasty as part of the traditional Chinese system of collecting so-called tribute from neighboring countries included as many as four or five hundred people who often remained in Okinawa for six months. During their stays they were housed in Kumemura, which became famous as a settlement of Chinese. The tribute system that brought these large groups continued in effect until the eighteenth century.

But it was not the only source of Chinese in Okinawa, because group of permanent immigrants too settled in Kumemura— families of what became known as the thirty-six names. Among the immigrants were many Buddhist—and especially Zen Buddhist—priests who were very important in the development of Okinawan martial arts.

Such Chinese martial arts as kempo were cultivated intensively and widely in Zen Buddhist temples because, in certain periods of Chinese history, the priesthood was constantly forced to protect itself from foreign invaders and from members of antagonistic sects. The Zen monks who immigrated into Okinawa naturally brought their native martial arts with them. These self-defense systems gradually blended with indigenous ones to become the distinctive Okinawa ancient martial-arts regimens.

Since it was customary in Chinese martial arts to practice unarmed combat and armed combat and armed fighting at the same time, it is likely that the Chinese systems brought to Okinawa in early times included implements like the nunchaku and the tonfa. Although some people argue that these two weapons were devised by the Okinawans on the basis of their own agricultural tools, it is more probable that their prototypes are to be found in the *shuang-chin-kin* (*so-setsu-kon* in Japanese) and the *shao-tse-kun* (*sho-shi-kon*). Among the weapons used by Chinese Zen priests were two called the *san-ku-ch'u* (*san-ko-sho*) and the *wu-ku-ch'u* (*go-ko-sho*), originally symbols of strength against the enemies of Buddhism. The san-ku-ch'u is the forerunner of the sai.

Not all of the ancient Okinawan martial arts derive from Chinese originals. The use of staffs is probably the oldest kind of Okinawan native weapon. A book called *One Thousand Years of Okinawan History* (*Okinawa Issennen-shi*) mentions a copy of a staff used by one of the Okinawan lords in 1314. The people of Okinawan villages probably often took up staffs to protect themselves and their homes when they heard the sound of the warning horn signifying that bandits were making another of their not infrequent raids. Moreover, it is recorded that beating with staffs was a punishment for adultery and other immoral acts. It is unclear how and when the staff altered its role from that of an implement of punishment and defense to the weapon of the *jo-jutsu* branch of the ancient Okinawan martial arts. It is easy to trace the development of the use of the scythe however, since this was the only blade implement permitted to Okinawan farmers. They naturally incorporated it as a weapon in their martial training.

Up to this point, I have suggested two reasons for the paucity of ordinary weapons among the people of Okinawa: the scarcity of metal in the islands and the prohibition against weaponry imposed by the governmental dynasty of rulers. But is it possible that these two explanations fail to cover the entire picture. It may well be that the wealth of materials obtained by the people through local agriculture and foreign trade and the high level of their cultural and political society made the Okinawans a nation of peace-loving people without the need or the desire for weapons. They did not, after all, resist the invasion of the Shimazu clan of Kyushu, when they invaded and conquered the Okinawan islands.

In 1816 a man named Basil Hall sailing on a ship carrying an English envoy traveled to Kanton, Korea, and Okinawa. After he returned to Europe, he had an interview with Napoleon, who is said to have sneered coldly when informed that the people of Okinawa had no weapons of any kind, not even swords and bows. "What do they fight with, then?," Napoleon is said to have retorted. Nor is it surprising that the French general should have found the Okinawan lack of weapons startling since his was a time when all of Europe was plunged into a series of costly and bloody wars. A pacific people who need no weaponry must have seemed strange indeed to him.

As their dealings with the Shimazu conquerors from Japan show, the Okinawans were a people who preferred and found it necessary to solve problems in a peaceful fashion. And the martial arts of the Okinawans—including the use of the nunchaku and sai and karate—are designed solely for the purposes of self-defense.

Nunchaku

As the preceding section on Okinawan history reveals, the history of the development of armed and unarmed combat in the Ryukyus is uncertain and vague. The same is naturally true of the nunchaku, but it likely that the Chinese who immigrated from China in the thirteenth and fourteenth centuries brought their knowledge of fighting staffs with them. The Okinawans may have heard about these combat techniques and may have gone to the Chinese settlement in the village of Kumemura to learn. They may have been instructed in the Chinese methods and may then have used their own knowledge to modify what they learned to suit their own needs and situation.

The derivation of the Okinawan word *nunchaku* too is unclear, though it is almost certain that the two Chinese weapons called the shuang-chin-kun and the shao-tse-kun are its forerunners. Whereas the Okinawan nunchaku consists of two rods (octagonal in cross section) connected by means of a cord, the Chinese shuang-chin-kun consisted of two round rods connected by means of metal fitting. There were several varieties of the weapon. In one, both rods were the same length; one rod was held in one hand so that the other rod could swing freely. In another version, one rod was longer than the other. The longer rod was held in both hands, and the shorter one was used to strike the head of an opponent who was protecting himself with a shield. The weapon was cleverly designed so that even should the person weilding it make a bad strike, the short rod would not swing back and strike his hand. Still another version—called the san-chin-kun consisted of three rods connected by metal fittings.

The rods of the nunchaku must be of a hard, tough wood that can withstand powerful strikes. In the past and today oak is the most popular material, though ebony and iron wood are used because of their heaviness. Hard woods, which in the past were considered especially valuable, are effective in nunchaku; but they have the unfortunate tendency to be brittle and to break easily. Heavy woods are good and will enable you to progress in nunchaku techniques, but you must choose weights that are compatible with your own strength.

In modern nunchaku silk or nylon chords are used to connect the two rods; in special cases, iron chain is used. But in Okinawa in the past, horse tail and sometimes a vine called *kanda* was the material for this purpose. The kanda vine has great significance for the people of Okinawa, as it was considered magic and was often employed in festival celebrations. The cord must be tied so that there are from eight to nine centimeters between the attached ends of the rods. If the cord is too long, the swing of the rod will be irregular. If it is too short, it may break as a result of friction. Because of this danger, always check the cords connecting the rods of the nunchaku before use. Sometimes the rods are carved for the sake of ornament or to prevent the hand from slipping on them. Or a hole may be drilled in the end of one of the rods so that it makes a whistling sound when whirled.

Because of the danger of serious injury from a rod that flies loose during practice, you must always buy nunchaku from manufacturers whose products are completely reliable. In my training hall, I ask the students to use nunchaku made by the Tokaido Company, Ltd., whose merchandise, fortunately, is exported to most parts of the world. It is most unadvisable to make your own nunchaku. If you must make your own, give maximum consideration to safety.

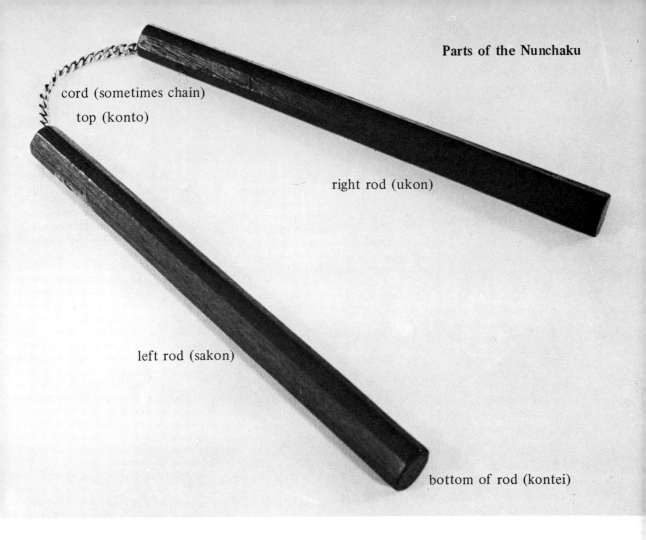

cord (sometimes chain)

top (konto)

right rod (ukon)

left rod (sakon)

bottom of rod (kontei)

Characteristics

The nunchaku is made of simple materials. It is portable, light, and convenient to handle, though it is capable of delivering powerful blows within a fairly wide range of space. Under ordinary circumstances, the nunchaku is held in one hand and swung up and down, forward and backward, right and left. Its movement takes advantage of the power generated by centrifugal force to execute strikes and other techniques that protect the body of the person wielding the weapon. Although the one-hand swinging method takes maximum advantage

of the characteristics of the nunchaku there are other special techniques as well. For example, the top (konto) or the bottom tip (kontei) of one of the rods may be used in thrusts and strikes. In addition, both rods may be used in a kind of pincers attack; the cord binding the rods can be wrapped around some part of the opponents body; or both rods may be used to gether in strikes and thrusts. The possibility of using the weapon in one-hand or two-hand techniques of the basic kind and of the several variation kinds described above make the nunchaku an implement of great versatility.

13

Sai

As has been explained earlier, metals are extraordinarily scarce on the Okinawan islands. It is therefore almost a certainty that any metal implements found in the ancient Okinawan martial arts were introduced from China. Although, as is the case with the nunchaku, details of the times and ways in which the sai was brought into the country are not known, it is probable that Chinese priests trained in martial arts were the first to bring it to Okinawa.

The weapons employed by these priests were usually sturdy, practical versions of the many implements found in ancient Indian and Chinese icongraphy as used in protecting Buddhism. The sai, for instance, is said to have evolved from the sword held in the hand of Indra, a great Hindu god who was incorporated into Buddhism as a protective deity.

The sai as found in Okinawa of the distant past was somewhat different from one used in modern martial arts. The metal part was entirely flat; the tsuka was made by using split bamboo tied in place with cords. The shape of the yoku and of the tsuka varied to suit the convenience of the owner. The tip of the monouchi and the end of the tsukagashira were often sharpened to fine points. Since this practice results in an extremely dangerous weapon, it is never followed today. The modern sai form is very much standardized. For the sake of safety the monouchi is a pipe either round or octagonal in cross section. The metal parts are chromium-plated. In selecting a sai, be sure the metal is tempered to prevent it from bending or breaking easily. Choose a weapon of weight that suits your own physique. The length of the sai that is most compatible with your body size can be determined in this way. Lay your

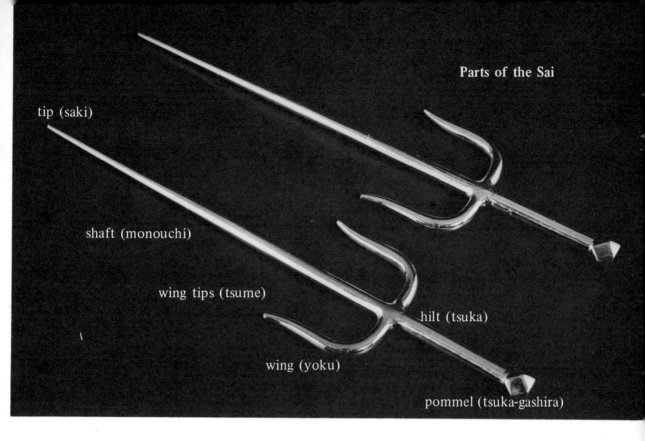

Parts of the Sai

tip (saki)

shaft (monouchi)

wing tips (tsume)

hilt (tsuka)

wing (yoku)

pommel (tsuka-gashira)

index finger along the tsuka. The base of the finger should be placed at the base of the yoku. When your finger is in this position, its tip should just reach the tsuka-gashira, and the monouchi should extend two or three centimeters beyond your elbow. To prevent the hand from slipping, the tsuka must be wrapped in thick cord or thin leather thongs.

Characteristics

The distinctive form of the sai consists of a shaft, called the monouchi, from the base of which spread to curving, hornlike projections called the yoku or wings. In addition, at the base of the yoku is a hilt or tsuka. The sai is held by this hilt and is swung in all directions in both attack and defense movements. Sometimes a pair of sai are used together. The sai may be held in the ordinary fashion (honte-mochi) or in a reverse position (gyakute-mochi). Blocks are the major technique, though thrusts and strikes with the monouchi and blocks, thrusts, and hooks with the wings two are possible. For all of the sai techniques strong, limber wrists are very important. Because sai techniques help develop these traits in the wrists, karate men have often used them as supplementary training.

nunchaku

Stances (tachikata)

Although there are no definite stances in the ancient Okinawan martial arts, the most effective and useful defense attack karate stances are used in nunchaku and sai training. The stances shown here are essential to good nunchaku and sai techniques. They must be mastered because the accuracy and instantaneous power needed for nunchaku and sai work depend on the stance. Your stance must be stable enough to enable you to block and withstand attacks, but it must be flexible enough to allow you to react quickly and to make whatever changes are necessary to conform to changing situations. The ancient Okinawan martial arts sometimes require that the weapon be moved with complete freedom through given distances; this means that the stance must allow completely harmonious movement of the weapon.

2

soto-hachiji-dachi

The heels are aligned and are separated by a distance roughly equal to the width of the shoulders. Because it is the preparedness stance, the soto-hachiji-dachi allows you to conform to whatever attack may be forthcoming (#2).

musubi-dachi

1

3

zenkutsu-dachi

One heel is forward; the two heels are about the width of the shoulders apart. The forward knee is slightly bent. This stance is best used when attack or defense must be made in the forward direction (#3).

The heels are brought together so that they touch lightly. This stance is used at the beginning of a technique (#1).

side view

shiko-dachi

The heels are about the width of the shoulders apart, and both knees are bent. This stance is convenient for movements to the right or to the left (#4).

neko-ashi-dachi

One foot is advanced. The heels are aligned and are about the length of two feet apart. The weight of the body is on the rearward foot; the forward heel is raised slightly in constant preparedness. Although, at a glance, it seems unstable, the neko-ashi-dachi is excellent for attack and defense because of the mobility it permits (#5).

5

side view

shumoku-dachi

The feet are wide apart, the heels are aligned, and both knees are bent. The rearward foot supports slightly more weight than the forward foot. (Note that the feet are farther apart than in the neko-ashi-dachi.) This stance is used mainly in defense (#6).

kokutsu-dachi

Both feet are wide apart, the forward and backward heels are aligned, and both knees are lightly bent. The head is turned to the rear. This stance is used mainly in defense (#7).

side view

side view

sagi-ashi-dachi

Only one foot is on the ground in this stance, which allows rapid transition from defense into attack or from attack into defense (#8).

Positions (kamae)

The kamae, are of the greatest importance to all the martial arts because, without them, no amount of technical skill or bodily strength will enable you to protect yourself or to attack with the necessary speed and accuracy. The kamae must be a harmonious blend of all three of the following elements: feeling (mental attitude), spirit (judgment), and strength (technical skill). No one of the three must be allowed to overshadow the others.

Ma-ai (interval) is of importance to the kamae. Ma-ai, too, involves three different, but intimately related, elements: time, space, and the psychological nature of the situation. The English translation *interval* might be interpreted to mean that one must assume a fixed spatial relation with the opponent and never alter it. But this clearly is not the case, since one must face all kinds of opponents, armed and unarmed, fast and slow, skillful and unskilled, keen and dull, large and small. The proper interval, therefore, changes with each opponent and with each situation. In addition, you must continually alter the interval between you and the opponent to keep yourself always in an advantageous position. When you are about to strike, close the interval. When you are forced to evade the opponent's strike, increase the interval. Knowing how to do this requires great concentration and study.

Another major point in kamae is the way in which you direct your gaze. There have been many interpretations of the best way to direct the glaze, but the important points are these. You must never fix your eyes. You must keep a constant watch on the movements of the opponent. You must be always aware of the nature of the environment and of everything that is taking place around you.

Finally, breathing, too, must be taken into consideration. It is impossible to judge your own actions and those of the opponent with detachment and calm if your breathing is irregular and disturbed.

1

ichimonji-gamae

The nunchaku is held in a straight line above the head. The kamae is called a right kamae when the right foot is forward and a left kamae when the left foot is forward.
(Note: for phonetic reasons the word *kamae* becomes *gamae* in combination with other words.)

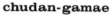

chudan-gamae

The nunchaku is held in front of the chest (#2).

gedan-gamae

The nunchaku is held at the level of the right kneecap. The right leg is advanced (#3).

gyaku-waki-gamae

This is very much like the waki-gamae except that the nunchaku is held in a straight line at the side of the body on the same side as the advanced foot (#5).

waki-gamae

The nunchaku is held extended in a straight line at the side of the body. When it is on the right side, the kamae is called a right kamae (#4).

gyakute-waki-gamae

The nunchaku is gripped in the reverse (gyaku) position (both thumbs are on the outside). The nunchaku is held in a straight line at the side of the abdomen (#6).

muso-gamae

The left hand is raised to the left side of the face, and the right hand holds the other nunchaku rod at the left armpit (#7).

katate-muso-gamae

One rod of the nunchaku is held in one hand. This rod rests on the shoulder of the same side; the other rod is held under the armpit from behind (#8).

9

10

hiji-kakoi-gamae

The name means that the nunchaku itself surrounds one elbow (in this case the right elbow). The position is achieved by holding one rod of the nunchaku in the right hand, which is held ·at the left side of the face. The other rod is held in the left hand, which is at the right armpit. The nunchaku itself forms a right angle (#9).

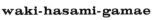

waki-hasami-gamae

One rod of the nunchaku is held in one hand. The other is held in the armpit (#10).

11

kane-gamae

The left hand, holding one of the nunchaku rods, is held at the left side of the face; the right hand, holding the other rod, is held in front of the right armpit. The nunchaku itself forms a right angle (#11).

12

haimen-gamae

The nunchaku is held in a straight line across the back (#12).

koshi-gamae

The nunchaku, both rods of which are gripped in a reverse (gyaku-te, thumbs outward) fashion, is held behind the body so that it wraps forward around the hips (#13).

katate-chudan-gamae

Both rods of the nunchaku are gripped in one hand and are held at the height seen in the ordinary chudan-gamae (#15).

katate-gedan-gamae

Both rods of the nunchaku are held in one hand at the height seen in the ordinary gedan-gamae (#16).

maki-gamae

The arms are crossed in front of the chest, and the nunchaku is held so as to wrap around the neck (#14).

25

morote-waki-hasami-gamae

morote-muso-gamae

morote-kane-gamae

tenchi-gamae

26

Basic Swings (kihon-furi)

To master the basic furi, first practice remaining in one position. Then practice as you move about. Finally, combine several of the swings in continuous motions until you are able to employ them with complete freedom.

Since the nunchaku consists of two rods connected by a cord, the slightest mistakes in the bend of the wrist or the twist of the elbow in manipulating can cause it to fall short of its mark or to be less effective than it ought to be. In nunchaku techniques, the proper interval, body movement, twists of the hips and wrists, extension and contraction of the joints, and bodily strength determine success. Only when all of these aspects of the execution of the techniques are in harmony can one expect the nunchaku to manifest its greatest power.

Moving economically from the kamae into the furi is of the greatest importance. The furi must be one that follows easily and naturally from the kamae of the moment. From the beginning of the furi until the nunchaku strikes its mark, you must pay attention to the action and power of the hips, shoulders, elbows, and wrists. Ordinarily, after the furi strike, the swinging end of the nunchaku returns to the hand that held it. Sometimes, however, it is allowed to swing naturally behind the hips. Or it may be quickly stopped or allowed to move naturally into the next furi.

1   2   3

yoko-ichimonji-furi

This swing moves the nunchaku rod on a horizontal line in front of the face. Extend the elbow well and make use of the twisting motion of the hips to increase the power of the attack. If the swing is too wide, it will destroy the balance of the body and greatly reduce the power of the attack. In addition, it will make it difficult to catch the swinging rod of the nunchaku. As a variation, it is possible to swing the rod above the head two or three times before stopping it. Accurate and careful catching of the nunchaku is very important and deserves intense study and frequent review.

Begin in the ichimonji-gamae in the soto-hachiji-dachi (#1). With the right hand, swing the nunchaku forward so as to pull the rod from the left hand (#2). Allow the nunchaku to swing naturally; do not stop it short (#3). Catch the nunchaku with the left hand (#4). At the moment at which you stop one rod, with the left hand, swing the nunchaku so as to pull the other rod from the right hand (#5–#6). Catch the swinging rod with the right hand (#7). Repeat the series several times.

Movement Practice

This is a combination of the preceding swing with foot movement. In practice with movement, balance in the body and in the weapon and the stance and the way the feet are moved are of great importance. No matter how skillful the swing, if the body is out of balance, the attack will lose its effect; of course, balance without good swing is ineffectual too. In other words, the nunchaku and the body must act in harmony together. After you have mastered all of the swings introduced in the following pages, practice them thoroughly in combination with body movement.

Begin in the shiko-dachi and the ichimonji-gamae. With the right hand, pull the rod of the nunchaku from the left hand and, at the same time advancing the right foot, swing the nunchaku with considerable force (#1 and #2). Maintaining the stability of your hips will greatly increase the power of the

1

2

3

4

nunchaku swing (#3). Without stopping it short, allow the nunchaku to swing naturally (#4). As you assume the shiko-dachi, catch the nunchaku with your left hand (#5). Following the same procedure, repeat the series with the left foot advanced and using the left hand.

5

6

7

8

ichimonji-suihei-furi

This technique resembles the yoko-içhi-monji-furi (p. 29) except that the swinging hand does not rise above the head, but travels to a position in front of the chest. This means that the catching hand must move in keeping with the flow of the nunchaku to reach the diagonal rear side of the head. The swinging hand must move in a scooping-rising motion.

Begin in the ichimonji-gamae. With the right hand, pull the rod of the nunchaku from the left hand and swing it forward and diagonally downward (#1 and #2). Swing to generate maximum power with the nunchaku (#3). Without stopping the nunchaku short, allow it to move naturally until it is caught by the left hand (#4 and #5). Following the same general procedure, swing the nunchaku with the left hand (#6—#9). Repeat the series several times.

hachiji-furi

This technique has a wide range of applicability. It can be used to force the opponent's attack down. Then with a twist of the wrist, it can be converted into an attack. When swinging the nunchaku downward, you must extend the elbow; when swinging it upward, however, you must pull the elbow to your side. If repeated several times so that the nunchaku describes a figure 8 in front of you, this technique can develop very strong wrists.

1

2

3

4

5

6

7

8

Begin in the zenkutsu-dachi and the muso-gamae. With the right hand, swing the nunchaku over the shoulder and downward on a diagonal line to the left (#1 and #2). Swing the nunchaku all the way down in the diagonal left direction (#3). In a circular motion, swing the nunchaku upward in the diagonal left direction (#4). From the diagonal left, swing the nunchaku downward to the diagonal right (#5 and #6). In a circular motion, swing the nunchaku upward to the diagonal right (#7). From the upper right, continue swinging down to the left (#8 and #9).

Steps 2 through 9 are an unbroken series. Practice to be able to execute this series with either the right or the left hand. When stopping the nunchaku, allow it to swing naturally and catch it in your armpit (waki-gamae; #11 and #12).

kote-gaeshi-furi

The proper stopping and catching of the nunchaku are the major points of emphasis in this swing. The nunchaku must not be forced to stop its movement unnaturally. Instead, the swinging hand must guide it easily to the hand that will catch it. It is necessary to repeat the swing many times at increasing speeds in order to develop the skill to manipulate the nunchaku with complete ease. Sometimes the nunchaku is swung in two or three rotations; sometimes it is stopped in a special way; and sometimes, vertical swings are alternated with horizontal ones.

10

9

8

Begin in the right zenkutsu-dachi and the left waki-gamae. At the instant when one rod of the nunchaku leaves the left hand, turn the right wrist to swing the nunchaku directly forward (#1 and #2). In a circular motion, move the right hand so as to swing the nunchaku upward (#3). After the nunchaku has made a complete circle, catch it in the left hand (#4). Next, release the rod from the right hand and turn the left wrist so as to swing the nunchaku directly forward (#5). In a circular motion, turn the left wrist so that the nunchaku swings upward (#6). After the nunchaku has made a complete circle, catch it in the right hand (#7). Repeat the series again (#8 and #9), increasing speed as you continue the technique.

6 7

katate-kote-gaeshi-furi

In this technique the same hand swings and catches the free rod of the nunchaku. It is difficult to execute without much patient training. When catching the free rod, you must hold the thumb of the receiving hand out-stretched wide or it will be caught between the nunchaku rods. You will find that mastering this technique will greatly improve your ability to use the nunchaku.

Begin in the right zen-kutsu-dachi and the left waki-gamae (#1). As the left hand releases one of the nunchaku rods, turn the wrist of the right hand so as to swing the nunchaku to the front (#2). In a circular motion, swing the nunchaku upward with the right hand (#3). Catch the nunchaku with the right hand (#4). Once again, turn the wrist so as to swing one rod of the nunchaku forward (#5).

Repeat steps #2 through #4 several times (#6—#8) until you can perform this technique with complete ease with either the right or the left hand.

shamen-gaeshi-furi

This swing, which leads the nunchaku on a diagonal downward line, is a basic technique used in both defense and attack. The nunchaku must descend on a diagonal, wrap around the hips, and stop at the buttocks. Unless this is done properly, the free rod may strike you in the back. After the nunchaku has wrapped round the hips, you must swing it quickly forward again so as to be prepared to move smoothly into the next technique.

Begin in the right zenkutsu-dachi and the chudan-morote-gamae (#1). Raise the right hand to the right side and the left hand to the right shoulder (#2). Swing the right hand forward so that it pulls the nunchaku rod from the left hand and swings it forward (#3). Swing the nunchaku downward to the diagonal left (#4). Allow the nunchaku to wrap around your hips (#5). Use the twisting motion of the wrist to swing the nunchaku forward to the right again (#6). (See kote-gaeshi, p. 36). Catch the nunchaku in the left hand (#7).

41

waki-gaeshi-furi

The most important points in this technique are the twist of the wrist, the extension of the elbow, the opening of the armpit to allow the nunchaku to return to its original position, and the closing of the armpit after the nunchaku has returned to that position. Unless the action of the wrist and the elbow are correct, the free rod of the nunchaku can strike your elbow or the side of your abdomen. Variations call for allowing the nunchaku to travel to the armpit on the opposite side of the body or for allowing it to make two or three full turns before stopping in the armpit.

Begin in the right zenkutsu-dachi and the right waki-hasami-gamae (#1). Extend your right elbow so as to draw the rod of the nunchaku from your right armpit (#2). When the nunchaku has swung outward as far as it can go, twist your wrist to bring the free rod back to its original position (#3). Open your right arm so that the nunchaku can return to the right armpit (#4). The moment the nunchaku is under the right armpit, bring the right arm close to the right side of the body (#5).

tate-ichimonji-furi

In this technique, the nunchaku is swung in a wide circle straight forward and is then suddenly stopped and swung back to its original position under the right armpit. The nunchaku must be stopped suddenly and swung upward quickly to prevent it from striking the swinging hand. In addition, accurately catching the upward-swinging nunchaku in the hand or in the armpit is important. Practice and repeat the technique enough to give you full freedom with it.

Begin in the zenkutsu-dachi and the katate-muso-gamae or the muso-gamae (#1). Swing the nunchaku straight forward and down by lowering your right arm parallel to your body (#2–#4). Stop the nunchaku suddenly when it has gone as far forward as possible (#5). Raise it immediately to the right shoulder (#6 and #7). Open your right arm outward away from the body so that the free rod of the nunchaku can swing under it from behind (#8). When the nunchaku has moved into the armpit, bring your right arm immediately to your side to hold the nunchaku in place and assume the

katate-muso-gamae (#9). It is possible to catch the free rod of the nunchaku in the left hand, which must be brought to the right armpit. This method will put you in the muso-gamae.

muso-kaeshi-furi

All of the techniques explained so far have called for swinging the nunchaku downward. This one, however, calls for swinging it upward, allowing it to cross the shoulder, and catching it with the opposite hand. The hand that catches the nunchaku rod must then be prepared to move into the next technique. The timing of the turn of the wrist must be accurate, or the nunchaku will move on an irregular course. Sometimes, the nunchaku is allowed to swing backward over the shoulder without first having been swing forward. No matter which method you chose, however, you must practice to be equally proficient with the right and the left hand.

Begin in the right zenkutsu-dachi and the right muso-gamae (#1). Swing the nunchaku upward and to the front in a line leading to the diagonal left (#2). At the left diagonal front position, twist your left wrist so that the back of the left hand faces outward (#3). Swing the nunchaku so that it falls beyond the left shoulder (#4). Catch the nunchaku in the right hand after it has crossed the left shoulder. This will put you in the left gyaku-muso-gamae (#5). When repeated training in this technique has given you a degree of proficiency, speed up your motions.

haimen-kaeshi-furi

Concealing the weapon behind your back, you prevent the opponent from knowing what you are about to do until you swing the nunchaku upward from your hips in a scooping motion. Since it is sometimes possible to swing the nunchaku downward from the shoulder, this technique has many subtle applications to both attack and defense. When the nunchaku is swung behind your body, the elbow of the swinging hand must be stable, or the other hand will be unable to catch the rod easily.

1

2

3

Begin in the left zenkutsu-dachi and the left haimen-gamae (#1). With the right hand, swing the nunchaku diagonally upward and forward (#2). It must rise still farther upward and diagonally to the left (#3). Swing the nunchaku wide upward and diagonally to the right (#4). Swing it downward to the diagonal left. The nunchaku must wrap around your hips (#5). Turn your wrist so that the nunchaku travels upward and to the diagonal right (#6 and #7). Using your left hand, catch the nunchaku behind your back. This will put you in the right haimen-gamae (#8). Practice beginning with the left and with the right hand.

8

7

6

4 5

gyakute-hachiji-furi

The nunchaku rods are gripped so that the thumbs of the hands are turned inward. Then one rod is swung in front of the body in a figure-eight motion. The subtle turn of the wrist at the moment of the swing is of the greatest importance. Mastering this technique will mean a great step forward in the use of the nunchaku.

Begin in the left zenkutsu-dachi and the koshi-gamae (#1). Using the left hand, swing the nunchaku directly to the right side (#2). In a circular movement, swing the nunchaku diagonally upward to the right (#3). Immediately swing the nunchaku downward to the diagonal left (#4). In a circular motion, swing the nunchaku upward to the diagonal left then swing it down again to the diagonal right (#5 and #6). The nunchaku must now wrap around your hips.

Catch it in your right hand at the right side of your body (#7). It is possible to use this variation method. The wrist is turned so that the nunchaku returns to its original position (#8). Next the nunchaku is wrapped around your hips from the left and your right hand (thumb turned inward) catches it at your left side (#9 and #10).

1 2 3

morote-furi

Begin in the right zenkutsu-dachi and the morote-muso-gamae
(#1). Simultaneously swing the nunchaku held in the right
hand diagonally downward to the left and the one held in
the left hand diagonally downward to the right (#2). As they
swing the nunchaku downward, the arms cross in front of
your chest (#3). In circular motions, swing the right hand
diagonally upward to the left and the left hand diagonally
upward to the right (#4). Continue by swinging the right
hand downward diagonally to the left and the left hand
diagonally downward to the right (#5). Using the twisting
action of the wrists, swing both nunchaku to a level higher
than the shoulders (#6). Next, swing both nunchaku forward
and straight out. When they have swung as far as possible,
use the twisting action of the wrists to bring the free ends of
the nunchaku to the armpits (#7). When the nunchaku are
in the armpits, bring both arms close to the body to pin
the rods in place and to assume the morote-waki-hasami-
gamae (#8). In a variation of this technique, beginning at
#6, bring both arms down parallel to the sides of the body
and stop the nunchaku when they have swung as far to the
rear as possible (#9). Immediately swing the nunchaku
upward to a level higher than the shoulders (#10). When the
nunchaku have swing as far as possible to the rear and have
wrapped around to enter the armpits pin them in place at
once by bringing your arms close to your body (#11). This is
performed according to the directions for the tate-ichimonji-
kaeshi-furi (p. 44).

9
10

4 5   6

7

8

11

Nunchaku Kumite

A right muso-gamae against the opponent's jodan-gamae (#1). When the opponent attacks in the gedan position, lifting your right foot, swing the nunchaku downward with the right hand and allow his weapon to pass in front of you (#2). Immediately swing the nunchaku upward (#3). Advancing on the right foot, strike the opponent in the head (#4). It is possible to strike him on the right side of the head (#5).

Ichimonji-gamae against the opponent's jodan-gamae (#1). When the opponent attacks from the jodan position, withdraw your left foot and swing the nùnchaku to the side (#2). Immediately swing the nunchaku upward and, at the same time, advance the left foot diagonally (#3). As you move your body forward, strike the opponent on the wrist (kote) (#4).

The chudan-gamae against the opponent's chudan-gamae
(#5). When the opponent attacks in the chudan position,
turn your body to the left and block his weapon (#6).
Immediately swing the nunchaku upward (#7). Strike the
opponent in the knee (#8).

Right chudan-gamae against the opponent's chudan-gamae (#1). When the opponent attacks in the jodan position, retract your left foot and block his weapon with a muso-gamae (#2). Turning your body to the left, quickly swing the nunchaku upward with your right hand (#3). Strike the opponent in the face (#4).

Haimen-gamae against the opponent's chudan-gamae (#5). When the opponent attacks your right foot, lift your foot and, swinging the nunchaku downward with the right hand, block his weapon (#6). Immediately swing the nunchaku upward (#7). Stepping forward on the right foot, strike the opponent in the head (#8).

The ichimonji-gamae against the opponent's chudan-gamae (#1). When the opponent attacks in the gedan position, block his weapon with the rod you hold in your left hand (#2). He will then move into an attack in the jodan position. When he does, move your body to the left and, at the same time, quickly swing the nunchaku upward with your right hand (#3). Strike the opponent in the head (#4).

Kane-gamae against the opponent's chudan-gamae (#5). When the opponent attacks in the jodan position, withdraw your right foot and block his weapon with the hiji-kakoi-gamae (#6). At the same time, turn your body to the right and allow his weapon to pass your body. With the left hand, swing the nunchaku upward (#7). Strike the opponent in the knee (#8) or in the hip (#9).

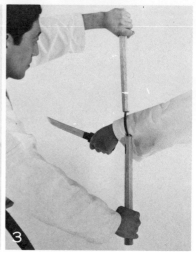

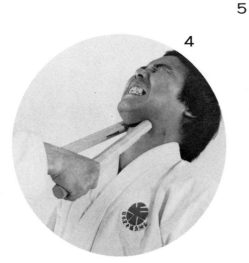

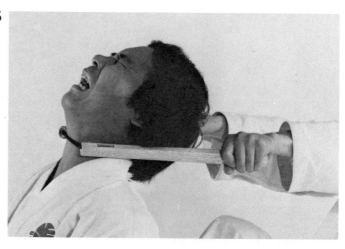

some other techniques

Blocking by crossing the rods of the nunchaku and stopping the attack with the connecting cord (#1).

Blocking by thrusting forward with both rods and pressing the connecting cord against the opponent's arm (#2).

Holding the two rods in a vertical straight line and blocking with the connecting cord (#3).

Thrusting both rods into the opponent's throat (#4).

Pinching the opponent's neck between the two rods (#5).

Pinching the opponent's wrist between the two rods (#6).

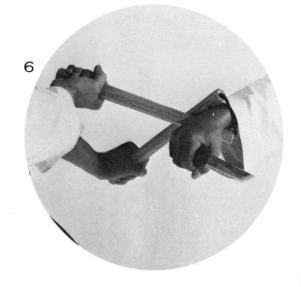

7

9

8

Pinching the opponent's wrists between the two rods (#7).

Striking with the bottoms of the two rods (#8).

Striking with the bottom of one rod (#9).

Thrusting with the bottom of one rod (#10).

10

Striking with one rod (#11).

11

12

Thrusting both rods into the opponent's abdomen (#12).

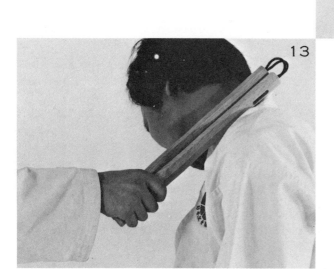

13

Striking with both rods held in one hand (#13).
Striking with both rods held together and parallel in both hands (#14).

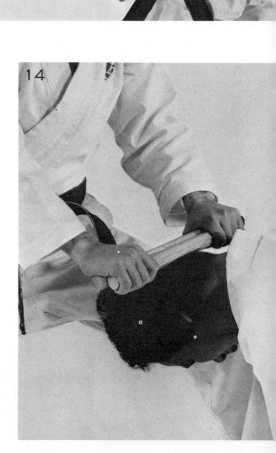

14

15   16

The opponent grips the wrist of the hand
holding the nunchaku (#15).
Breaking the opponent's hold and con-
trolling his arm by swinging the nunchaku
around from the inside (#16).
The opponent uses both hands to grip the
wrist of the hand holding the nunchaku
(#17).
Breaking the opponent's hold and con-
trolling his arm by swinging the nunchaku
around from the outside (#18).

17

18

Using the right gedan-gamae against the opponent's attack from the jodan (#1). Block the opponent with the nunchaku rod you hold in your left hand (#2). Pivoting on the left foot, turn your body to the left. At the same time, quickly swing the nunchaku upward with the left hand (#3). Strike the opponent's head with the nunchaku (#4)

1

2

3

4

Holding both rods of the nunchaku in one hand, block the opponent who attacks in the chudan position (#1). When the opponent attacks in the chudan position, retracting your left foot, block his left wrist with a parrying movement of the nunchaku (#2). Quickly swing the nunchaku upward (#3). Strike the opponent's face (#4)

1 2

5

6

7

The left chudan-gamae against the opponent's chudan-gamae (#1). When the opponent attacks in the chudan position, turn your body to the left and block his arm by holding the nunchaku in a straight, vertical line (#2). Quickly swing your right hand around and wrap the nunchaku connecting cord around the opponent's wrist (#3). Force the opponent off balance by lifting him with the nunchaku. Kick the opponent's knee with a right sokuto (#4).

In a variation of this technique, when the opponent advances his right foot and assumes the chudan-gamae, turn your body to the left and block his arm with the nunchaku (#5). Quickly raise the nunchaku above your head (#6). With the bottoms of both rods, strike the back of the opponent's head (#7).

You are in the left gedan-gamae and are facing your opponent (#1). The opponent draws a short sword and tries to attack you. He is in the jodan position. At this time, crouch by leaning forward (#2). When the opponent steps toward you, thrust the tips of the nunchaku rods into his throat (#3).

You are facing the opponent and are in a left waki-gamae (#4). He begins to attack in the chudan position. Croach and cause his attack to miss. When you do this, strike the opponent's left knee with the nunchaku, which you are holding in your left hand (#5). When your opponent falls forward, swing the nunchaku upward (#6). When he has fallen, execute an uchikomi to his back (#7).

5

4

A left chudan-gamae against the opponent's chudan-gamae (#1). When the opponent attacks in a chudan position, turn your body to the left and block his weapon with both nunchaku rods (#2). Quickly swing the nunchaku upward (#3). Lean your upper body forward and turn it to the left (#4). In a rising, scooping motion, swing the nunchaku into the opponent's abdomen (#5) or into his genitals (#6).

6

The maki-gamae against the opponent's chudan-gamae (#1). When the opponent attacks in the jodan position, raise both hands and block with the left nunchaku rod (#2). Immediately, step forward slightly as if you were going to bring your body into contact with his (#3). Thrust the bottoms of the nunchaku rods into the opponent's forehead (#4).

As an alternate, at #2 you may turn your body to the left and allow his weapon to pass you on the right side (#5). You may then strike him in the head with the bottom of the left rod (#6).

Or, at #5, you may turn your body to the left and, at the same time, releasing your hold on the right nunchaku rod, with your left hand, swing the nunchaku around so that the free rod strikes the opponent in the face (#7 and #8).

The opponent is in the chudan-gamae, and you are in the left chudan-gamae (#1). When the opponent attempts to attack in the chudan position, turn your body to the left and block his weapon to the right with the connecting cord of the nunchaku (#2). Quickly turn the nunchaku with your right hand so that its connecting cord wraps around the opponent's sword. In this way force him off balance (#3). At the same time put your right foot behind the opponent's right foot (#4). Trip him with the foot and cause him to fall (#5). Swing the nunchaku upward with your right hand and execute an uchikomi to his side (#6 and #7).

The ichimonji-gamae against the opponent's
chudan-gamae (#1). In this case, you initiate
the attack. Swinging your hips around and
taking advantage of the force this action
generates, direct the nunchaku toward the
opponent's face. He blocks this by moving the
staff he is using as a weapon directly to the
side (#2). At this stage, if you strike it at
the right place, the opponent's weapon may
break. Immediately leap to avoid the opponent's
attempted sweep-attack on your fcot (#3).
You may swing the nunchaku downward and
strike the opponent on the head as you land
after the jump (#4—#6).

4

5

6

Morote-kane-gamae (one nunchaku held in each hand) against the opponent's chudan-gamae (#1). When the opponent begins an attack in the jodan position, assume a defensive posture as you retract your right foot. Block his weapon with the two nunchaku held crossed (#2 and #3). At the same time, as you allow his weapon to pass by you to the left, raise your right hand (#4). As you strike him on the back with the right nunchaku, swing the left one upward and then strike him on the back with it (#5 and #6).

3

4

5

6

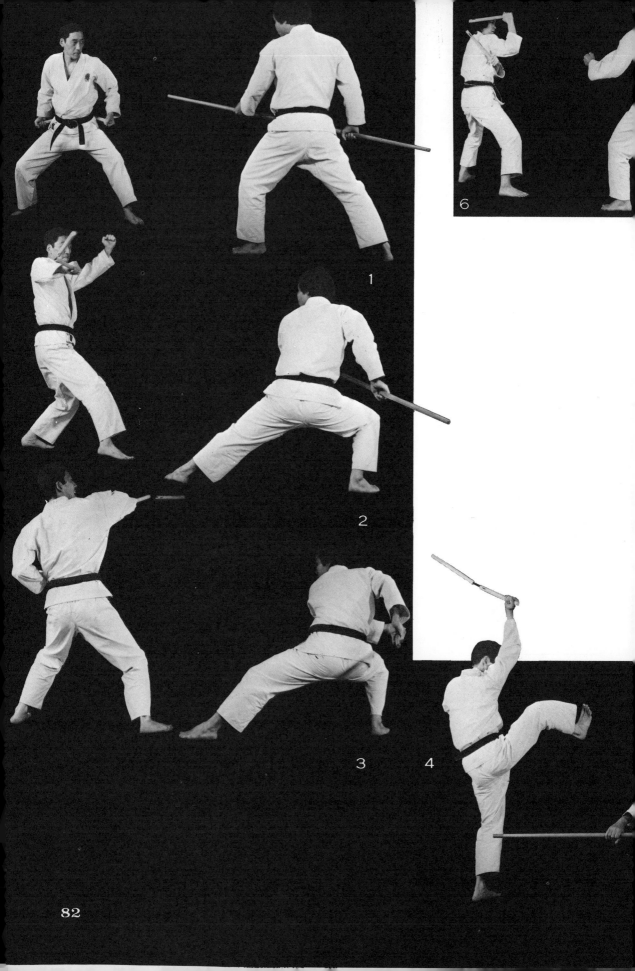

1

2

3　　4

6

Koshi-gamae against the opponent's chudan-gamae (#1). Initiate an attack by stepping forward on your left foot. Holding the nunchaku in the right hand, thumb outward, strike toward the opponent's face (#2). The opponent will crouch to protect himself and will then immediately attempt to sweep your right foot with his weapon (#3 and #4). Raise your right foot and then, stepping forward on that same foot, strike the opponent's head with the nunchaku (#5).

Muso-gamae against the opponent (#6). When the opponent attacks in the chudan position, retract your right foot and strike him in the wrist with the nunchaku, which you hold in your right hand (#7). Raise the nunchaku again and strike him again in the neck (#8 and #9).

The opponent grips your right hand, in which you hold the nunchaku (#1). Immediately retracting your right foot, bring the nunchaku toward your body and grip its top ends in your left hand (#2). Crouching slightly, bring your left hand forward to pin the opponent's wrist (#4). When you have extended your left hand forward as far as it will go, release it from the nunchaku. Immediately swing the nunchaku upward with your right hand and strike the opponent on the back with it (#5 and #6).

1

2

3

The opponent grips both your arms from the front (#1). Immediately retracting your right foot, swing both arms to the left and upward. At the same time, grip the upper ends of the nunchaku from below in your left hand (#2). Pull the nunchaku toward you and turn your body to the right (#3). Continuing to turn your body, force your opponent to fall, and swing both arms free (#4). At the same time, swing the nunchaku upward with your right hand and strike the opponent in the side with it (#5 and #6).

1

6

86

2

3

4

5

The opponent has wrapped one arm around your right arm and is trying to take away the nunchaku you are holding in the hand of the same arm (#1). As you pull the nunchaku with your left hand, turn your body by bringing your left foot behind your right foot (#2). Pulling the nunchaku still farther forward and downward, continue turning your body and throw the opponent (#3 and #4). Pull the nunchaku free and swing it upward with your right hand. Strike the opponent in the side with the nunchaku (#5 and #6).

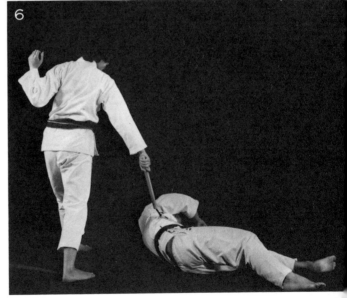

The opponent has gripped your collar from the front in his right hand (#1). Immediately transfer the nunchaku from your right hand to your left hand over the opponent's arm (#2). Retracting your left foot and crouching on your left knee, pull the nunchaku toward you and in this way pin the opponent's right elbow (#3). Raise the nunchaku above your head and, with the middle of the rods, strike the opponent in the head (#4 and #5).

4 5

The opponent has wrapped his arms around you from behind (#6). Crouching slightly, advance your right foot to the right diagonal front. At the same time, break free of the opponent's arms by raising both your arms (#7). Turn your body by bringing your left foot behind your right foot; raise the nunchaku in your right hand (#8). At the instant when you have turned completely around, strike the opponent in the side with the nunchaku (#9).

8 9

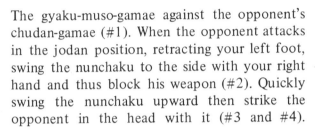

The gyaku-muso-gamae against the opponent's chudan-gamae (#1). When the opponent attacks in the jodan position, retracting your left foot, swing the nunchaku to the side with your right hand and thus block his weapon (#2). Quickly swing the nunchaku upward then strike the opponent in the head with it (#3 and #4).

You and the opponent are kneeling in the formal position facing each other (#5). The opponent takes his weapon in his hands and rises slightly on his knees in preparation for an attack in the jodan position. You take the nunchaku in your right hand and assume a defensive posture (#6). You block the opponent's attack. Immediately, swing the nunchaku upward with your right hand (#7). After blocking the opponent's attack in this way, immediately swing the nunchaku upward with your right hand (#7 and #8). Strike the opponent in the head with the nunchaku (#9).

Basic Nunchaku Kata

Mastery of certain basics is essential to nunchaku training as to any other martial-arts training. To make this mastery easier to attain and to arrange training in a more rational fashion, famous martial arts masters of the past devised formalized patterns of motions. These patterns are called the kata. Although in earlier times there were more kata than exist today, inadequate organization among instructors and faulty ways of keeping records have resulted in the loss of many. Some of the kata are named for the martial-arts master who originated them; others are named for geographical places.

It is the duty of all of use who are devoted to the martial arts to see that this priceless heritage from the past is preserved. We can best do this by understanding the kata thoroughly. This means not merely knowing the order and ways in which they are performed, but grasping their inner spiritual meaning and studying constantly to discover the best ways to put them to use. Unless the person practicing them has so completely assimilated their spirit that their movements come to him as a matter of reflex, truly living kata cannot be expected.

In this book I present a basic nunchaku kata devised by my honored teacher Shinken Taira and revised by me, since there is no traditional kata especially for the nunchaku alone. In addition, I offer the Tawada sai basic kata. I trust that both will be of interest and value to the student of this branch of the martial arts.

Points of Caution in Kata Training

1. Practice each kata often and accurately.
2. Understand the meaning of each movement.
3. Master the technical aspects of each kata.
4. Maintain constant balance.
5. Breathe calmly at all times.
6. Keep your eyes on your target at all times.
7. Remember that your spiritual drive must continue in full force until after the conclusion of each movement.
8. Accurately abide by the given motion lines in turns, advances, and retreats.
9. All of the actions involving the weapon must be smooth.

1

2

nunchaku kata

3

Standing in the musubi-dachi, hold both rods of the nunchaku in your right hand. Both arms hang naturally at your sides. Your eyes must look naturally and calmly forward.

• Remaining in this portion, bow to the front.

• Raise your head and return to the original position. These three steps are the opening phases of the execution of the kata.

1. Assume the sotohachi-ji-dachi by moving your left foot directly to the left. Bring the nunchaku to the front of your body and hold it with both hands.

2. Raise the nunchaku over your head in a straight horizontal line; assume the ichimonji-gamae.

3. Taking one step to the rear on your left foot, assume the shumoku-dachi; at the same time, from a left kamae, switch to a right chudan-gamae.

4. Move your right elbow inward toward the center of your body and bring your right hand to the left front side of your face. At the same time, bring your left hand to your right armpit to assume the right hiji-kakoi-gamae.

5. Taking one step forward on your left foot, assume the left shumoku-dachi. At the same

4

time, from a right kamae, switch to a left chudan-gamae.

6. Bringing your left elbow inward, lift your left hand to the right side of your face. At the same time, draw your right hand to your left armpit to assume the left hiji-kakoi-gamae.

7. Taking one step forward on your right foot, assume the shumoku-dachi. At the same time, from a left kamae, switch to a right chudan-gamae.

8. Bringing your right elbow to your right side, bring your left hand to the left diagonal front of your face to assume a right-kane-gamae.

By retracting your right foot, assume the right neko-ashi-dachi. Bringing your right elbow inward, move your right hand to the right side of your face. At the same time, draw your left hand to your right side to assume the muso-gamae. Retract your right foot to put yourself in the right zenkutsu-dachi. At the same time, swing the nunchaku downward to the left diagonal front with your right hand. Then in a round motion, swing it diagonally upward to the left. Next swing it diagonally downward to the right and then upward diagonally to the right. Next swing it diagonally downward to the left again. These movements are the hachiji-furi (see p. 34).

10. At the left side of your body, catch the nunchaku in your left hand; assume the left waki-gamae.

11. Pivoting on your right foot, step to the left foot, to assume the left shumoku-dachi; at the same time, assume the left chudan-gamae.

12. Bring your left elbow inward and move your left hand to the right side of your face. At the same time, draw your right hand to your left armpit to assume the left hiji-kakoi-gamae.

11 12

13. As you assume the shumoku-dachi by taking one step forward on your right foot, move into the right chudan-gamae.

14. Moving your right elbow to your right side, bring your left hand to a point diagonally to the left of and above your face. This wi'l put you in the right kane-gamae.

15. Retract your right foot to assume the right neko-ashi-dachi. Moving your right elbow inward, take your right hand to the right side of your face. At the same time, take your left hand to your right armpit to assume the right muso-gamae.

13

15   14

16. Sliding your right foot forward assume the right zenkutsu-dachi. At the same time, swing the nunchaku diagonally upward to the left with your right hand.

17. After allowing the nunchaku to wrap around your hips, use the twist or your wrist to pull it forward again. Catch the nunchaku in your left hand.

18. Pivoting on your left foot, turn your body 180 degrees to the right. As you assume the shumoku-dachi, put yourself in the right chudan-gamae.

19. Moving your right elbow inward, take your right hand to the left side of your face. At the same time, draw your left hand to your right armpit to put yourself in the right hiji-kakoi-gamae.

20. Sliding your left foot forward, assume the left shumoku-dachi. At the same time, move from a right kamae to the left chudan-gamae.

21. Drawing your left elbow to your left side, take your left hand to a point diagonally to the right of your face. This will put you in the left kane-gamae.

22. Retract your left foot to assume the left neko-ashi-dachi. As you do this, move your left elbow inward and take your left hand to the left side of your face. At the same time, bring your right hand to your left armpit to put yourself in the left muso-gamae.

21

22

20

23

23. Sliding your left foot forward to assume the left zenkutsu-dachi, swing the nunchaku downward to the diagonal right with your left hand. After allowing the nunchaku to wrap around your hips, use the twist of your wrist to swing it forward again.

24. Catch the nunchaku in your right hand.

24

25. Pivoting on your right foot, slide your left foot one step forward to assume the left shumoku-dachi. At the same time assume the left chudan-gamae.

26. Drawing your left elbow to your left side, take your right hand to a point diagonally to the right of and above your face to assume the left kane-gamae.

27. Retract your left foot to assume the left neko-ashi-dachi. Drawing your left elbow inward, take your left hand to the left side of your face. At the same time take your right hand to your left armpit to assume the left muso-gamae.

28. Sliding your left foot forward to assume the left zenkutsu-dachi, swing the nunchaku upward to the diagonal right with your left hand. This is the hachiji-furi.

29. After allowing the nunchaku to swing around your hips, use the twisting action of your wrist to swing it upward diagonally to the left. When it has gone behind your back, catch it in your right hand to assume the left haimen-gamae.

30. Immediately swing the nunchaku forward and upward with your right hand. Swing it wide from the left diagonal front to the right, then swing the nunchaku downward diagonally to the left.

31. Catch the nunchaku at your left side in your left hand to assume the left gyaku-waki-gamae.

32. Sliding your left foot one step forward to assume the right shumoku-dachi, assume the right chudan-gamae.

33

34

35

36

37

38

39

33. In this same position, draw your left elbow to your right side as you take your left hand to a point diagonally to the left of and above your head. This will put you in the right kane-gamae.

34. Drawing your right foot back, assume the right neko-ashi-dachi. Drawing your right elbow inward, take your right hand to the right side of your face. At the same time, pull your left hand to your left armpit to assume the muso-gamae.

35. Sliding your right foot forward to assume the right zenkutsu-dachi, swing the nunchaku downward diagonally to the left with your right hand (hachiji-furi).

36. After allowing the nunchaku to swing around your hips, use the twist of your wrist to swing it upward to the diagonal right. Catch it after it has swung behind your back; you will then be in the right haimen-gamae.

37. Immediately swing the nunchaku forward with your left hand. Swing it wide from the diagonal front right to the diagonal upper left. Then swing the nunchaku down diagonally to the right.

38. Catching the nunchaku in your right hand at your right side, assume the gyaku-waki-gamae.

39. Pivoting on your right foot, turn your body 270 degrees to the left. Assume the shumoku-dachi and at the same time, put yourself in the left chudan-gamae.

40

43

41

44

42

45

40. Drawing your left elbow inward, put your left hand at the right side of your face. Simultaneously, draw your right hand to your left armpit to assume the left hiji-kakoi-gamae.

41. Sliding your right foot one step forward, assume the right shumoku-dachi. At the same time, from a left kamae, switch to a right chudan-gamae.

42. As you bring your right elbow to your right side, raise your left hand to a point to the left of and above your face. This puts you in the right kane-gamae.

43. Retract your right foot to assume the right neko-ashi-dachi. Drawing your right elbow inward, lift your right hand to the right side of your face. At the same time, draw your left hand to your right armpit to assume the muso-gamae.

44. Sliding your right foot forward to assume the right zenkutsu-dachi, swing the nunchaku forward and downward with your right hand (tate-ichimonji-gaeshi-furi; see p. 44).

45. The nunchaku is resting on and hanging partly behind your right shoulder. This is the katate-muso-gamae.

46. Swing the nunchaku downward then further toward your right side and allow it to wrap around your hips. Using the twist of your wrist, swing the nunchaku forward again.

47. Catch the nunchaku in your left hand.

46

47

48. Pivoting on your left foot, turn you body 180 degrees to the right to assume the shumoku-dachi. At the same time, assume the right chudan-gamae.

49. Drawing your right elbow inward, raise your right hand to the left side of your face. At the same time, draw your left hand to your right armpit. This will put you in the right hiji-kakoi-gamae.

50. Sliding your left foot forward one step, assume the left shumoku-dachi. At the same time, from a right kamae, assume the left chudan-gamae.

51. In the same position, draw your left elbow

50   51   52   53

to your left armpit. At the same time, take your right hand to a point diagonally right of and above your face. This will put you in the left kane-gamae.

52. Retracting your left foot to assume the left neko-ashi-dachi, draw your left elbow inward. Raise your left hand to the left side of your face and at the same time draw your right hand to your left armpit to assume the muso-gamae.

53. Sliding your left foot forward to assume the left zenkutsu-dachi, swing the nunchaku downward and forward with your left hand. Immediately swing the nunchaku upward.

54

110

55

54. The nunchaku rests on your left shoulder and partly hangs down your back on the left side. This is the left katate-muso-gamae.

55. In this same posture, swing the nunchaku downward to the diagonal right. After allowing it to wrap around your hips, use the twist of your wrists to swing the nunchaku forward again. Catch it in your right hand.

front view

56

57

front view

58

56. Putting your weight on your right foot, slide your left foot forward one step to assume the left shumoku-dachi. At the same time, assume the left chudan-gamae.

57. Drawing your left elbow to your left side, raise your right hand to a point diagonal to the right of and above your face. This will put you in the left kane-gamae.

58. Retracting your left foot, assume the left neko-ashi-dachi. At the same time, draw your left elbow inward and raise your left hand to the left side of your left muso-gamae.

59. Sliding your left foot forward to assume the left zenkutsu-dachi, swing the nunchaku downward to the left with your left hand. After allowing the nunchaku to wrap around your hips, use the twist of our elbow to swing it upward diagonally to the right. After it has gone behind your back, catch it with your right hand to assume the left haimen-gamae.

60. Sliding your right foot forward one step, swing the nunchaku upward and to the front with your right hand. Swing the nunchaku wide from the left front to the upper right. Then swing it downward to the left again. At the same time, assume the right zenkutsu-dachi and allow the nunchaku to wrap around your hips. Then, using the twist of your wrist, swing the nunchaku upward to the diagonal right. When it has swung behind your back, catch it in your left hand for a right haimen-gamae.

60

61. Sliding your left foot forward one step, swing the nunchaku upward and forward with your left hand. Swing the nunchaku wide from the right diagonal front to the left upper diagonal. Then swing it downward to the right diagonal. Assume the left zenkutsu-dachi and, at the same time, allow the nunchaku to wrap around your hips. Next, using the twist of your wrist, swing it diagonally upward to the left. When it has swung behind your back, catch the nunchaku in your left hand for a left haimen-gamae.

61

62. Once again, sliding your right foot forward one step, swing the nunchaku upward and forward with your right hand. Swing the nunchaku wide from the left diagonal front to the upper right. Then swing it downward to the diagonal left. Assume the right zenkutsu-dachi and, at the same time, allow the nunchaku to wrap around your hips. Using the twist of your wrist, swing the nunchaku back to the front.

63. Catch the nunchaku with your right hand.

64. Pivoting on your right foot, turn your body to the left. As you assume the left shumoku-dachi, assume the left chudan-gamae.

65. Putting your weight on your right foot, draw your left foot back to the diagonal left till both feet are aligned. This will put you in the left kokutsu-dachi. As you take this stance, assume the right hiji-kakoi-gamae.

66. Bring your left foot to your right foot. Raise you left foot to assume the left sagi-ashi-dachi. At the same time,

front view

65

66

swing the nunchaku downward to the diagonal left with your right hand. Then swing it downward to the left and upward in a circular motion to the diagonal left and down to the

67

68

69

118

70

diagonal right again. Continue by swinging upward to the
diagonal right then downward to the diagonal left. Allow
the nunchaku to wrap around your hips. Bringing your right
foot to the floor again, assume the right zenkutsu-dachi, and
with a twist of your wrist, swing the nunchaku forward again.
67. As you assume the right zenkutsu-dachi, catch the
nunchaku with your left hand.
68. In the same position, turn to the rear and assume the
right kokutsu-dachi. At the same time, assume the left
hiji-kakoi-gamae.
69. Bringing your right foot to your left foot, raise your
left foot to assume the right sagi-ashi-dachi. At the same
time, swing the nunchaku downward to the diagonal right
hand. Continue by swinging first downward to the diagonal
right, then in a circular motion upward to the diagonal right,
then downward to the diagonal left, then upward to the
diagonal left. Finally, swing it downward to the diagonal
right and allow the nunchaku to wrap around your hips.
Putting your left foot back on the floor, assume the left
zenkutsu-dachi. Then with a twist of your wrist, swing the
nunchaku forward again.

119

70. As you assume the left zenkutsu-dachi, catch the nunchaku with your right hand.

71. Putting your weight on your right foot, draw your left foot to the rear. As you face forward and assume the right shumoku-dachi, assume the right chudan-gamae.

72. Drawing your right elbow inward, raise your right hand to the left side of your face. At the same time, draw your left hand to your left armpit to assume the right hiji-kakoi-gamae.

73. Sliding your left foot one step forward, assume the left shumoku-dachi. At the same time assume the left chudan-gamae.

74. Drawing your left elbow inward, raise your left hand to the right side of your face. At the same time, draw your right hand to your left armpit to assume the left hiji-kakoi-gamae.

75. Sliding your right foot forward one step, assume the right shumoku-dachi. At the same time, assume the right chudan-gamae.

76. Drawing your right elbow to your right side, raise your left hand to a point diagonally to the left of and above your face. This puts you in the right kane-gamae.

77. Retract your right foot to assume the right neko-ashi-dachi. At the same time, draw your right elbow inward and raise your right hand to the right side of your face. Draw your left hand to your right armpit to assume the right muso-gamae.

78. Sliding your right foot forward, assume the right zenkutsu-dachi. At the same time swing the nunchaku downward and forward with your right hand. Swing it down by

76

77

78

79

80

81

82

83

your right side, then immediately swing it up again. When the nunchaku crosses your right shoulder, catch it with your left hand to put yourself in the right muso-gamae.

79. Next, swing the nunchaku upward and to the left diagonal front with the left hand. Turn the left hand so that its top side faces outward and, twisting the wrist, swing the nunchaku above your left shoulder. When the nunchaku crosses your left shoulder, catch it in your right hand to assume the left gyaku-muso-gamae.

80. With your right hand, swing the nunchaku upward to the diagonal right then backward to the diagonal right. When it crosses your shoulder, catch the nunchaku with your left hand to put yourself in the right haimen-gamae.

81. Swing the nunchaku forward and upward with the left hand. Then swing it wide upward diagonally to the left and downward to the diagonal right. After allowing the nunchaku to wrap around your hips, use the twist of your wrist to swing it forward again.

81. Catch the nunchaku in your right hand.

82. Sliding your left foot forward one step, assume the left shumoku-dachi. At the same time assume the left chudan-gamae.

83. Bringing your left elbow to your left armpit, raise your right hand to a point diagonally to the right of and above your face to assume the left kane-gamae.

84

84. Draw your left foot back to assume the left neko-ashi-dachi. Drawing your left elbow inward, raise your left hand to the left side of your face. At the same time, bring your right hand to your left armpit to assume the left muso-gamae.

85. Sliding your left foot forward, assume the left zenkutsu-dachi. At the same time, swing the nunchaku downward and forward with your left hand. Turning your body to the left, quickly swing the nunchaku upward to the left. When the nunchaku has passed your left shoulder, catch it behind your back in your right hand to assume the left muso-gamae.

86. · Swing the nunchaku upward to the right with the right hand. Then, with the back of the right hand turned outward, twist the right wrist and swing the nunchaku upward to the diagonal right until it passes your right shoulder. When it has passed your shoulder, catch it behind your back in your left hand to assume the left gyaku-muso-gamae.

87. Next swing the nunchaku diagonally upward to the left in your left hand. Continue the swing till the nunchaku crosses your left shoulder. Catch it behind your back with your right hand to assume the left haimen-gamae.

85

86

87

125

88. Swing the nunchaku upward to the right in your right hand. Then swing it wide upward from the diagonal left to the diagonal right, and downward to the diagonal left. After allowing it to wrap around your hips, with a twist of your wrist, swing it forward again and catch it in your left hand.

89. Sliding your right foot one step forward, assume the right zenkutsu-dachi; at the same time assume the right ichimonji-gamae.

90. Swinging the nunchaku forward with your right hand, watch for an opportunity to act further. Then, pivoting on your left foot, turn your body all the way around to the left (counterclockwise). Still pivoting on your left foot, continue turning. Draw your left foot back to assume the shiko-dachi. At the same time, catch the nunchaku in your left hand to assume the right ichimonji-gamae. In other words, in #89 and #90, your body makes a complete 360-degree turn.

90

91. Drawing your right foot back, put your right knee on the floor to assume the right hiji-kakoi-gamae.

92. Swing the nunchaku downward to the right with the left hand. Then, after swinging it further downward to the diagonal right, make a circular movement to swing it upward to the diagonal right then downward to the diagonal left and upward to the diagonal left. Swinging it downward to the diagonal right again, catch it at your right side in your right hand. This puts you in the right waki-gamae.

93. Taking one step straight to the left side on the left foot, assume the soto-hachiji-dachi. Raise the nunchaku over your head in one straight horizontal line.

91

94. Bring your left foot to your right foot to assume the musubi-dachi. Lower both hands and hold the nunchaku in front of our body.

95. Take both rods of the nunchaku in your right hand and allow your arms to fall naturally at your sides.

96. Bow to the front then raise your head. This concludes the kata.

92

95

93

96

94

129

sai

Positions Used with the Sai

Employing the Sai

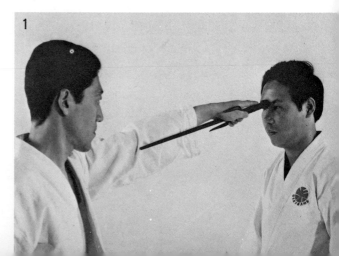

1

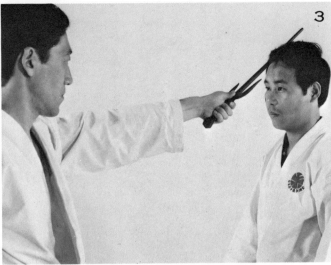

Thrust to the opponent's forehead with the tsuka-gashira of the sai (#1).

Thrust with the saki (tip) of the monouchi (#2).

Strike from above with the monouchi (#3).

Strike to the side of the head with the monouchi (#4).

Pull with the tsume (wing) (#5).

Driving thrusts with the monouchi of both sai. In addition, the tsume of the two sai are used to thrust still further (#6).

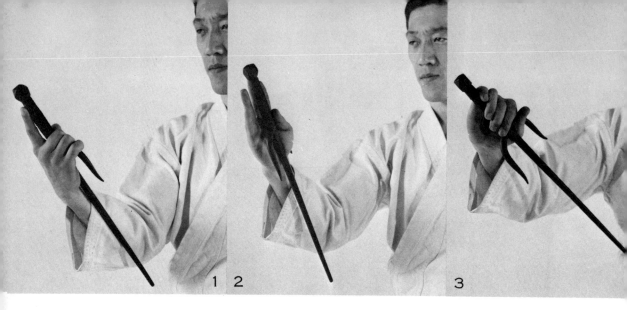

1   2   3

Basic Furi

The use of two sai as a pair is probably the outcome of Chinese influence. Since the sai are made of iron, they can deliver powerful blows. On the other hand, the weight of the metal means that great care must be exerted to execute the sai techniques with accuracy; any slovenliness in these techniques can lead to failure in attack or defense. Obviously, intense study must be devoted to mastering the sai techniques. Correct use of the fingers—especially the thumb—in the swings (furidashi) and conclusions (osame) is of great importance. In addition the twist of the wrist and the extension and flexion of the elbows to a large extent determine the success of sai attacks and defenses.

Hook your thumb under the yoku on the right and lay your index finger alone the tsuka so that it points to the tsuka-gashira. The other three fingers wrap around the left yoku from above (#1).
Leaving your thumb in the same position, bring all four fingers together along the tsuka (#2). Wrap the four fingers around the tsuka (#3). Grip the tsuka and pull the bottom toward you. This will point the tip of the monouchi away from you (#4).

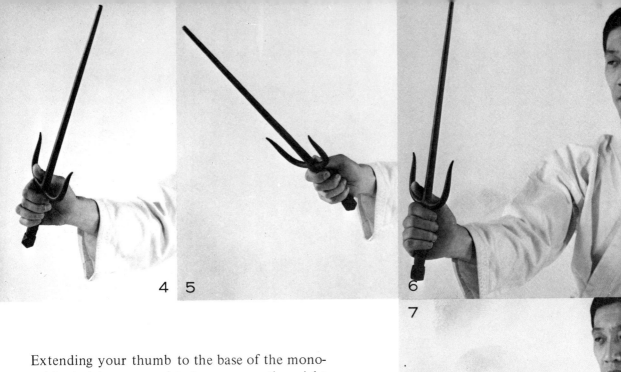

4 5 6

7

Extending your thumb to the base of the mono-uchi, twist your wrist to assume the right chudan-uchi. (In this position, the part of the weapon gripped in the hand becomes the center around which the tip of the monouchi is employed in uchikomi (#5).

Slide your thumb through the right yoku (#6). Resting the right yoku in the crotch between the thumb and the index finger, return the tip of the monouchi to its original position (#7). Release the tsuka and bring all four fingers to the top of the left yoku (#8).

Return the sai to its original position (#9).

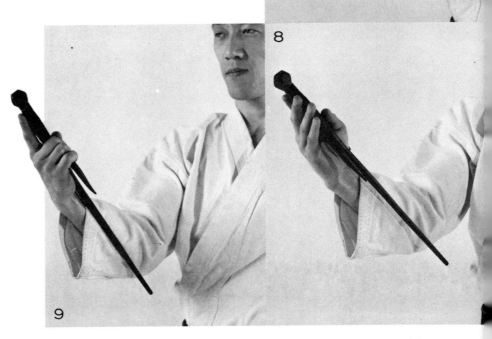

8

9

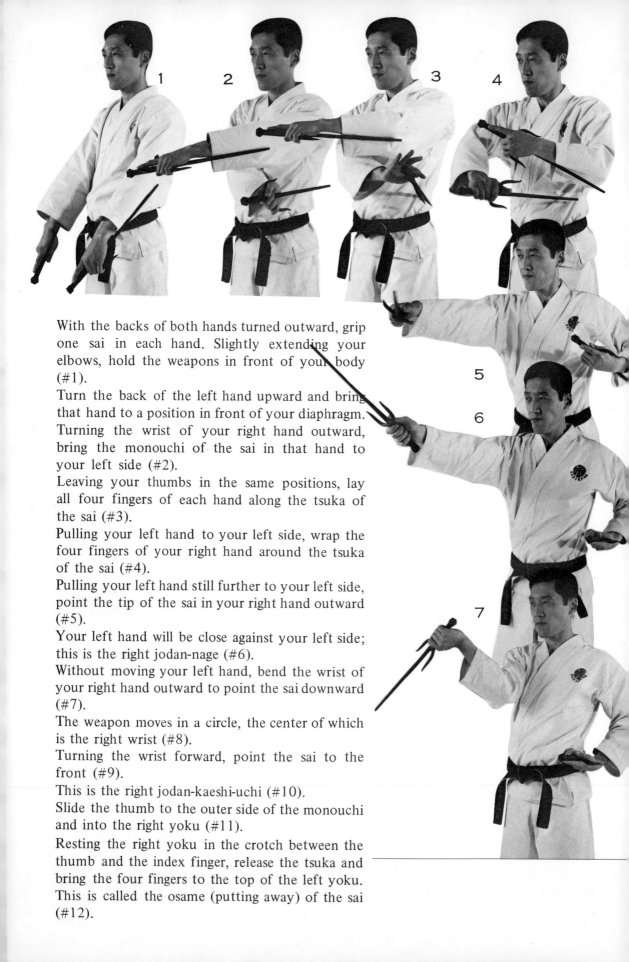

With the backs of both hands turned outward, grip one sai in each hand. Slightly extending your elbows, hold the weapons in front of your body (#1).

Turn the back of the left hand upward and bring that hand to a position in front of your diaphragm. Turning the wrist of your right hand outward, bring the monouchi of the sai in that hand to your left side (#2).

Leaving your thumbs in the same positions, lay all four fingers of each hand along the tsuka of the sai (#3).

Pulling your left hand to your left side, wrap the four fingers of your right hand around the tsuka of the sai (#4).

Pulling your left hand still further to your left side, point the tip of the sai in your right hand outward (#5).

Your left hand will be close against your left side; this is the right jodan-nage (#6).

Without moving your left hand, bend the wrist of your right hand outward to point the sai downward (#7).

The weapon moves in a circle, the center of which is the right wrist (#8).

Turning the wrist forward, point the sai to the front (#9).

This is the right jodan-kaeshi-uchi (#10).

Slide the thumb to the outer side of the monouchi and into the right yoku (#11).

Resting the right yoku in the crotch between the thumb and the index finger, release the tsuka and bring the four fingers to the top of the left yoku. This is called the osame (putting away) of the sai (#12).

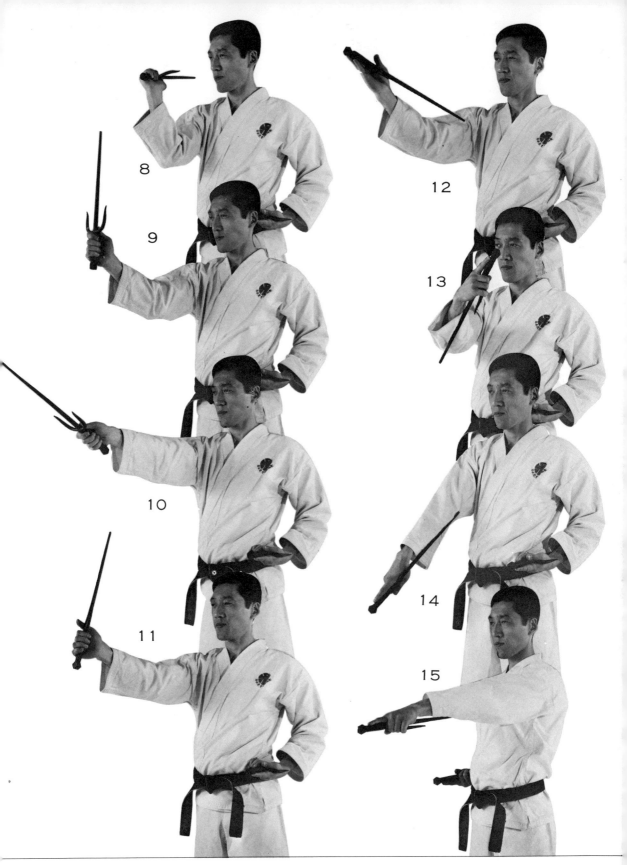

In a round movement, of which the elbow is the center, rotate the tsuka-gashira of the sai in a semicircle (#13).

This is the right gedan-harai-uke (#14). Next execute a left chudan-tsuki (#15).

137

Sai Kata

• With both sai in the right hand turned so that the tsuka-gashira points down, stand in the musubi-dachi with arms hanging naturally at your sides and with eyes turned forward. Bow to the front. Raise your head and return to the original position. These three steps constitute the opening of the kata. These three steps constitute the opening of the kata.

1. Bring the sai forward and hold them in both hands.
2. Taking one step directly to the left on the left foot assume the soto-hachiji-dachi. According to the method used in the yoko-uke, turn the backs of both hands to the front and lightly bend both elbows. Raise your forearms so that the sai are brought to a position in front of your chest.
3. Cross your arms, bringing the sai to your sides. Lower the sai. Allow your arms to hang naturally at your sides.
4. Sliding your left foot forward one step, assume the left zenkutsu-dachi. Assume the left chudan-kake-uke. At the same time bring your right hand to your right side.
5. Sliding your right foot forward one step, assume the right zenkutsu-dachi. Assume the right jodan-nage-uke and bring your left hand to your left side.
6. Sliding your left foot forward one step, assume the left zenkutsu-dachi. Assume the left jodan-nage-uke and bring your right hand to your right side.

1

2

7. Sliding your right foot forward one step assume the right zenkutsu-dachi. Assume the right jodan-nage-uke and bring your left hand to your left side.

8. Describing a semicircle with the weapon, turn the monouchi of the sai upward and bring it under your right arm (osame). While doing this execute a right gedan-barai-uke.

9. Next execute a left chudan-tsuki.

10. Then execute a right chudan-jun-zuki.

11. Drawing your right foot back to assume the right neko-ashi-dachi, turn the back of your right hand upward. Your right forearm should fall at about the position of your diaphragm. The sai in the right hand should form a cross with the sai in the left hand. This is called the left horan-gamae.

12. Making a circular movement (from inside outward) with your right foot, turn the back of your right hand upward and, making a circular motion, pull your right hand to your right side.

13. Sliding your right foot forward, assume the right zenkutsu-dachi. Execute a morote-jodan-tsuki.

14. Drawing your right foot back to assume the musubi-dachi, cross the sai above your head and execute a jodan-kosa-uke.

15. Sliding your right foot forward to assume

13

16

front view

15

14

the right zenkutsu-dachi, execute a morote-jodan-uchi.

16. Pivoting on your left foot, turn your body 180 degrees to the left. Assume the left zenkutsu-dachi and execute a morote-jodan-uke.

141

17

18

front view

front view

front view

19

20

front view

front view

17. Lifting your forearms, turn the sai tips upward and place them under your arms (osame).

19. Execute a right chudan-tsuki.

20. Execute a left chudan-tsuki.

21. Sliding your right foot one step forward, assume the shiko-dachi and execute a left gedan-barai. Turning its back inward, bring your right hand to your forehead.

22. Sliding your right foot forward diagonally to the right, assume the right zenkutsu-dachi and execute a right gedan-barai.

front view

23. Execute a left chudan-tsuki.
24. Execute a right chudan-tsuki.
25. Sliding your right foot forward diagonally to the right, assume the shiko-dachi and execute a right gedan-barai. Turning its back inward, bring your left hand to your forehead.
26. Stepping forward on your right foot, assume the right zenkutsu-dachi and execute a right jodan-nage-uke.
27. Sliding your left foot one step forward, assume the left zenkutsu-dachi and execute a left jodan-nage-uke.
28. Sliding your right foot forward one step, assume the right zenkutsu-dachi and execute a right jodan-nage-uke.
29. In a semicircular motion, turn the point of the monouchi upward and bring the sai under your arm (osame); execute a right gedan-barai.
30. Execute a left chudan-tsuki.
31. Execute a right chudan-tsuki.

front view
26

144

front view

27

28

29

30

31

front views

145

32

front view

33

34

35

36

front view

front vi

146

37

38

39

40

41

32. Drawing your right foot back to assume the right neko-ashi-dachi, turn the back of your right hand upward, bring that hand to your left side. Your right forearm will come to a position in front of your diaphragm. The two sai must intersect to form a cross at this point. This is the left horan-gamae.

33. Make a circle (from the inside outward) with your right foot. Turning its back to face outward, describe a large semicircle with your right hand then draw it to your right side.

34. Sliding your right foot forward, assume the right zenkutsu-dachi and execute a morote jodan-tsuki.

35. Drawing your right foot to your left foot, assume the musubi-dachi. Cross the sai above your head; this is the jodan-kosa-uke.

36. Sliding your right foot forward, assume the right zenkutsu-dachi and execute a morote jodan-uchi.

37. Pivoting on your right foot, turn your body to the left (counterclockwise) 180 degrees. Assume the left zenkutsu-dachi and execute a morote-gedan-uke.

38. Raise your forearms and extend your elbows slightly to bring the sai under your arms with points downward (osame).

39. Execute a left gedan-barai.

40. Execute a right chudan-tsuki.

41. Execute a left chudan-tsuki.

42

45

43

46

44

47

48

49

50

51

42. Putting your weight on your left foot, slide your right foot forward to assume the right zenkutsu-dachi. Execute a right jodan-nage-uke.

43. Drawing your right foot back, assume the right neko-ashi-dachi and execute a right jodan-kaeshi-uchi. As you assume a posture preparatory for a driving thrust, slide your right foot forward to assume the right zenkutsu-dachi. Execute a richt jodan-uchi.

44. Turning the sai point upward and putting it under your arm (osame), execute a right gedan-barai in a semicircular movement.

45. Execute a left chudan-tsuki.

46. Execute a right chudan-tsuki.

47. Pivoting on your right foot, turn your body 180 degrees to the left. Assume the left zenkutsu-dachi and execute a left jodan-nage-uke.

48. Retract your left foot to assume the left neko-ashi-dachi. Assume a position preparatory to the execution of a left uchikomi. Sliding your left foot forward, assume the left zenkutsu-dachi and execute a jodan-uchikomi.

49. Turning the tip upward and putting the sai under your arm, execute a left gedan-barai in a semicircular motion.

50. Execute a right chudan-tsuki.

51. Execute a left chudan-tsuki.

52

53

54

55

52. Pivoting on your left foot turn your body to the right execute a right jodan-nage-uke.

53. Sliding your left foot one step forward, assume the left zenkutsu-tachi and execute a left jodan-nage-uke.

54. Sliding your right foot one step forward, assume the right zenkutsu-dachi and execute a right jodan-nage-uke.

55. Turning the tip upward and bringing the sai under your arm (osame), execute a right gedan-barai in a semicircular motion.

56. Execute a left chudan-tsuki.

57. Execute a right chudan-tsuki.

58. Retract your right foot to assume the right neko-ashi-dachi. Turning its back upward, pull your right hand to your left side. Your right forearm should lie at a position in front of your diaphragm. The two sai should intersect each other at right angles. This is the left horan-gamae.

59. Swinging your right foot in a circle (from inside outward), turn your right hand back upward. In a large, forward, semicircular motion, bring your right hand to your right side. Sliding your right foot forward, assume the right zenkutsu-dachi and execute a morote-jodan-tsuki.

56

57

58

59

151

60. Bringing your right foot to your left foot, assume the musubi-dachi. Cross the sai and raise both of them over your head to execute a jodan-kosa-uke.

61. Sliding your right foot forward, assume the right zenkutsu-dachi and execute a morote-jodan-tsuki.

62. Pivoting on your right foot, turn your body 180 degrees to the left. Assume the left zenkutsu-dachi and execute a morote-gedan-uke.

63. Raise your forearms, and making use of the action of your elbows, turn the sai tips downward and bring them under your arms (osame).

64. Execute a left gedan-barai.

65. Execute a right chudan-tsuki.

66. Execute a left chudan-tsuki.

67. Putting your weight on your right foot, step back diagonally to the left rear on your left foot. Both feet will now be aligned and you should be in the right kokutsu-dachi. execute a right gedan-barai.

front view

60

61

62

63

front view

64

front view

65

front view

66

front view

67

68

68. Bring your left foot to your right foot. Assume the sagi-ashi-dachi and execute a right gedan-uke.

69. Lowering your right foot, assume the right zenkutsu-dachi. Turning the sai tip upward and bringing it under your arm (osame), execute a right gedan-barai in a circular movement.

70. Execute a left chudan-tsuki.

71. Execute a right chudan-tsuki.

72. Turning to the rear, assume the right kokutsu-dachi and execute a left gedan-barai. Turning its back inward, bring your right hand to your forehead.

73. Bring your right foot to your left foot. Assume the left sagi-ashi-dachi and execute a left gedan-barai.

70

69

71

74. Lowering you left foot, assume the left zenkutsu-dachi. Turning the sai point upward and putting it under your arm (osame), execute a left gedan-barai.

75

76

77

front view

75. Execute a right chudan-tsuki.

76. Execute a left chudan-tsuki.

77. Putting your weight on your left foot, bring your right foot to the right to assume a right zenkutsu-dachi. Execute a right jodan-nage-uke.

78. Sliding your left foot one step forward, assume the left zenkutsu-dachi and execute a left jodan-nage-uke.

79. Sliding your right foot one step forward, assume the right zenkutsu-dachi and execute a right jodan-nage-uke.

80. Turning the sai tip upward and putting it under your arm (osame), execute a right gedan-uke in a semicircular motion.

81. Execute a left chudan-tsuki.

front view

79

80

78

front view

front view

front view

81

front view

82

82. Execute a right chudan-tsuki.

83. Draw your right foot in to assume the right neko-ashi-dachi. Turning its back upward, bring your right hand to your left side. Your forearm should lie on a line adjacent to your diaphragm. The two sai should intersect at right angles. This is the left horan-gamae.

84. Turning your right foot in a circular motion (from the inside outward), make a wide, forward, circular motion with your right hand—back upward—as you bring it to your right side.

85. Sliding your right foot forward, assume the right zenkutsu-dachi and execute a morote-jodan-tsuki.

86. Bring your right foot to your left foot to assume the musubi-dachi. Cross the sai and bring them above your head to execute a jodan-kosa-uke.

87. Sliding your right foot forward, assume the right zenkutsu-dachi and execute a morote-jodan-tsuki.

88. Pivoting on your right foot, turn your body 180 degrees to the left. Assume the left zenkutsu-dachi and execute a morote-gedan-uke.

89. Raise your forearms, and using the action of you elbows, turn the sai, tips downward and put them under your arms (osame).

90. Execute a left gedan-barai.

84

front view

83

front view

85

front view

86

front view

87

front view

88

89

90

91. Execute a right chudan-gyaku-zuki.

92. Execute a left chudan-jun-zuki.

93. First bring your left hand under our right hand. Then quickly raise them both over your head and cross the sai to execute a jodan-kosa-uke.

94. Take a large step forward on your right foot. Drawing your left foot inward, assume the kosa-dachi. Turn the tip of the sai in your right hand upward and put it under your arm (osame). Bring it to your left side. In a wide movement to the left, raise the sai in your right hand above your head and execute a jodan-uchikomi.

95. Taking one step to the rear on your right foot, assume the shiko-dachi. Swinging the sai in the right hand rearward and the sai in the left hand forward, execute a chudan-uke.

96. Raise the sai in your right hand over your head in a side motion to the left. With the monouchi of the sai in your left hand, execute an uchiate.

97. Bringing your right foot to your left foot, assume the musubi-dachi. Execute tsukikomi with both the right and the left sai.

side view

96

side view

side view

98. Bringing your left foot to the rear, assume the shiko-dachi. Turning the tips of both sai upward and bringing them under your arms (osame), execute a left gedan-barai and a right chudan-yoko-uchi-uke.

99. Pivoting on your left foot, draw your right foot one step to the rear then turn your body 180 degrees to the right. Assume the shiko-dachi and execute a right gedan-barai and a left chudan-yoko-uchi-uke.

100. Bring your right foot to your left foot. Lift your left foot to assume the right sagi-ashi-dachi. Execute left gedan-barai-uke. Turning its back inward, bring your left hand to your forehead.

101. Bring your left foot to a position beside your right foot and assume the soto-hachiji-dachi. Turning the backs of both hands upward, lightly bend both elbow and raise your forearms to chest level.

102. Turning both sai in front of your chest, cross them. The allow both arms to fall naturally at your sides. Bring your left foot to your right foot to assume the musubi-dachi. Bring both sai forward. Put both in your right hand. Allow your arms to fall naturally at your sides and bow forward. Raise your head. This concludes the kata.

101

102

Sai Kumite

You are facing an opponent armed with a sword
(#1).
When the opponent attacks in the jodan position,
assume a defensive posture and retract your left
foot (#2).
Block his jodan attack with a right jodan-age-uke
(#3).
Allow his weapon to pass your body on the right
(#4).
Execute a left gyaku-zuki to his forehead (#5).

You are facing an opponent armed with a sword (#1).

When the opponent attacks in the jodan position, assume a defensive posture and retract your left foot (#2).

With both sai above your head, block his jodan attack with a jodan kosa-uke (#3).

Parry his weapon to the left with the left sai (#4).

With the right sai, execute an uchikomi to his face (#5).

You are facing an opponent armed with a staff (#1).
When the opponent attacks in the chudan position, raise your
right foot and parry his weapon with the sai in your right
hand (#2).
Next, when he attacks in the jodan position, turn your body
to the left and use a jodan-uke with the sai in your left hand
to parry his weapon (#3).
Allow his weapon to pass on the inward side of your body.
Swing the sai upward (#4).
With the sai in your left hand execute an uchikomi to his
face (#5).

You are facing an opponent armed with a sword (#1). When the opponent attacks in the chudan position, turn your body to the right and block and parry his weapon with the sai in your left hand (#2).

Immediately swing the sai upward (#3).

Execute an uchikomi to his face (#4).
Turn the tip of the sai in your left hand upward and bring
the sai under your left arm (#5).
At the same time, with the sai in your right hand, execute
a gyaku-zuki to the opponent's face (#6).

You are facing an opponent armed with a sword (#1).

When the opponent lifts the tip of his sword, catch it between the two sai and parry it to the left (#2).

Control his weapon with the sai in your left hand (#3).

When he attempts an attack in the jodan position, draw your left foot back. With both sai, block his weapon with a jodan-kosa-uke (#4).

Swinging both sai outward and upward, parry his weapon (#5).

Strike both sides of the opponent's body with the sai (#6).

With the tips of the yoku, execute a tsuki-komi (#7).

You are facing an opponent armed with a sword (#1).

When the opponent attacks in the jodan position, retract your left foot and, with the tsuka of the sai, execute a jodan-kosa-uke (#2).

Swinging both sai upward and outward, retract your right foot (#3).

Next, when he attempts an attack in the jodan position, turn your body to the left and block his weapon with the yoku of the sai in your left hand (#4).

Force his weapon downward and inward (#5).

Catch his weapon in the crotch of the yoku and raise it (#6).

Catch the opponent's side with the wing tips of the sai in your right hand (#7).

7

6

5